# A NOTE TO PARENTS

When your children are ready to "step into reading," giving them the right books—and lots of them—is as crucial as giving them the right food to eat. **Step into Reading Books** present exciting stories and information reinforced with lively, colorful illustrations that make learning to read fun, satisfying, and worthwhile. They are priced so that acquiring an entire library of them is affordable. And they are beginning readers with an important difference—they're written on four levels.

**Step 1 Books,** with their very large type and extremely simple vocabulary, have been created for the very youngest readers. **Step 2 Books** are both longer and slightly more difficult. **Step 3 Books,** written to mid-second-grade reading levels, are for the child who has acquired even greater reading skills. **Step 4 Books** offer exciting nonfiction for the increasingly proficient reader.

Children develop at different ages. **Step into Reading Books,** with their four levels of reading, are designed to help children become good—and interested—readers *faster*. The grade levels assigned to the four steps—preschool through grade 1 for Step 1, grades 1 through 3 for Step 2, grades 2 and 3 for Step 3, and grades 2 through 4 for Step 4—are intended only as guides. Some children move through all four steps very rapidly; others climb the steps over a period of several years. These books will help your child "step into reading" in style!

Step into Reading

# WHO SHOT THE PRESIDENT?

## The Death of John F. Kennedy

By Judy Donnelly

Illustrated with photographs

A Step 4 Book

Random House 🏠 New York

Photo credits: pp. 2, 4, 6, 7, 9, 12–13, 15, 16, 17, 18–19, 20, 33, 34, 38, 48, White House Photo Collection, John F. Kennedy Library; pp. 8, 42, copyright © 1967 by LMH Company. All rights reserved; pp. 10, 25, 26, 28, 43, AP/Wide World Photos; pp. 22, 36, 37, UPI/Bettmann Newsphotos; p. 31, copyright © 1963 by Bob Jackson, *Dallas Times Herald*.

Cover photo: UPI/Bettmann Newsphotos

*Library of Congress Cataloging-in-Publication Data:*
Donnelly, Judy. Who shot the president? (Step into reading. A Step 4 book) SUMMARY: Examines events surrounding the assassination of President Kennedy in 1963. Also discusses the Warren Commission findings and conspiracy theories. 1. Kennedy, John F. (John Fitzgerald), 1917–1963—Assassination—Juvenile literature. [1. Kennedy, John F. (John Fitzgerald), 1917–1963—Assassination] I. Title. II. Series: Step into reading. Step 4 book. E842.9.D66 1988 973.922′ 092′ 4 88-4418 ISBN: 0-394-89944-X (pbk.); 0-394-99944-4 (lib. bdg.)

Manufactured in the United States of America 1 2 3 4 5 6 7 8 9 0

STEP INTO READING is a trademark of Random House, Inc.

President and Mrs. Kennedy arrive in Dallas.

# Gunfire

*November 22, 1963. Dallas, Texas.*

A huge silver-and-blue plane touches down and comes to a stop. Crowds of people gathered at the landing field start to wave and cheer. A door opens. A handsome man climbs down from the plane. He is John F. Kennedy, the thirty-fifth president of the United States. A beautiful woman is beside him. She is his wife, Jacqueline.

The Kennedys greet crowds at the Dallas airport.

The President walks over to meet some of the crowd. Mrs. Kennedy is given a big bouquet of red roses. Then the Kennedys get into an open car. They are on their way to a special luncheon in their honor. John Connally, the governor of Texas, and his wife are riding with them. Other cars are filled with newspaper reporters, Secret Service agents, and important people such as Lyndon Johnson, the Vice President of the United States.

Slowly the line of cars moves through the city. All along the way crowds cheer and wave. Some of them hold up signs that read WELCOME JACK AND JACKIE and WELCOME JFK.

Mrs. Connally tells the President, "You sure can't say that Dallas doesn't love you today."

The car turns a corner and heads toward a highway. A little boy waves at the President. The President smiles and starts to wave back.

Thousands cheer the President during his ten-mile trip through the city.

Suddenly a shot rings out. The President clutches his throat. There is more gunfire. Governor Connally is hit. John Kennedy slumps over. His wife cries, "Oh, my God! They've shot my husband! Jack! Jack!"

Gunfire strikes down President Kennedy before anyone can help.

At the side of the road people scream and run. Two women throw themselves to the ground to keep from being hit. A mother tries to cover her child with her body.

A mother and father try to protect their children.

A Secret Service agent clings to the President's car as it speeds away.

The car behind the Kennedys' is full of Secret Service agents. Their job is to protect the President. One of them runs and leaps onto the Kennedys' car as it races to the nearest hospital.

Minutes later a news flash goes out. The President is wounded. How badly? No one knows.

It has been an ordinary Friday until now. Americans are at work or at school. They are shopping or eating lunch or playing ball. But everyone who hears the news stops. The word passes from person to person.

All over America crowds gather around television sets in stores or restaurants. People turn on radios in parked cars. Strangers stop one another in the streets. Everyone is stunned and shocked. Everyone wants to know, "Will the President be all right?"

At the hospital doctors try to save the President's life. Mrs. Kennedy waits nearby. Her pink suit is stained with her husband's blood. She is sure he is dying.

The Vice President of the United States, Lyndon Johnson, is there too. Secret Service agents guard him carefully. He will become president if John Kennedy does not live.

Finally the doctors can do no more. Mrs. Kennedy goes to her husband. She holds his hand and she prays.

In cities and towns everywhere millions of Americans are still waiting and hoping. Newscasters come on the air. Some of them weep as they say the words "The President of the United States is dead."

Ninety-nine minutes later Lyndon Johnson swears to serve as the thirty-sixth president

of the United States. Mrs. Kennedy stands
beside him. They are on a plane bound for
Washington, D.C. John F. Kennedy's coffin is
with them, in the rear of the plane just a few
yards away. Mrs. Kennedy is taking her husband home.

Lyndon Johnson is sworn in as president on the same plane that
took the Kennedys to Dallas only a few hours earlier.

# Remembering

People who lived through the day President Kennedy was killed sometimes think back. They can remember exactly where they were and what they were doing when they first heard the news. They remember their feelings of shock and sadness. It was a day like no other.

America had lost a president in a sudden, terrible way. But to so many Americans John Kennedy's death meant even more. It was like losing a close friend or a family member. They had probably never met Kennedy or even stood in the same room with him. But they loved him.

John F. Kennedy was the youngest man ever elected president. He was only forty-three years old when he moved into the White House. Everyone was fascinated with him and his family.

Here is the Kennedy family during the summer of 1962.

Mrs. Kennedy was beautiful and intelligent. Americans were proud of her. Wherever she went, crowds fought to get near her.

The Kennedys had two small children. Caroline was three and John Jr. was a newborn baby when their father took office. The President always called his son John-John.

President Kennedy plays with John-John and his toy horse on the White House porch. Once, Caroline's real horse trotted right into the White House.

The President's desk makes a good hiding place for Caroline and her friends.

Small children hadn't lived in the White House for many years. People loved to hear how the President made up stories for John-John. They loved to hear how Caroline played under her father's desk. They sent the children birthday cakes and presents. Stories and pictures of the Kennedys were everywhere.

John, who is on the right, was about two years old when this photo was taken. He is with his mother, his baby sister Rosemary, and his older brother Joe. John's parents always dreamed that one of their sons would become president. At first their hopes were pinned on Joe, not John. But that changed when Joe died in World War II.

John Kennedy himself seemed very special. He grew up in Massachusetts in a large, close family. He had eight brothers and sisters. John's great-grandparents were poor when they came to America from Ireland, but John's father became very rich. John F. Kennedy could have chosen to do anything. But he decided to serve his country.

John is at the upper left, with his mother and father and seven of his eight brothers and sisters.

To many Americans, John Kennedy was like a hero in a legend. He was handsome and strong. He was brave. He had been a real hero in World War II. The small patrol boat he commanded in the Pacific was wrecked at sea. One of his men was hurt. The enemy was close. Sharks filled the water. But John took the man's life jacket in his teeth and swam miles to an island, pulling his friend behind. He won a medal for his courage.

John Kennedy is at the wheel of his patrol boat.

After the war he wrote a book about a different kind of courage—the courage to do what is right even if everyone is against you. It was called *Profiles in Courage,* and it won America's most important prize for writing, the Pulitzer. When he was only twenty-nine, John Kennedy became a congressman. Later he was elected senator, and finally president in 1960. The vote was very close, but after he took office he became more and more popular.

John Kennedy served as president for less than three years—only about a thousand days. It wasn't long. But he made that time seem like a new beginning for America.

When he was sworn in as president, he said, "Ask not what your country can do for you—ask what you can do for your country."

He wanted people all over the world to have better lives. He gave ordinary Americans a special way to help. He began the Peace Corps, which sent thousands to live and teach in poorer countries.

John F. Kennedy stirred the nation with the speech he gave after he was sworn in as president.

He tried to make laws that would give blacks the same rights as whites.

He helped put the first American in space. He promised that the first man to reach the moon would be an American.

Most of all, he wanted a safe world. He said this was a president's most important job. Countries were testing nuclear bombs in the air, bombs that spread deadly radiation over the whole world. They were a terrible threat to the future.

Kennedy worked for an agreement. Over one hundred nations promised to stop above-ground tests of these bombs. Kennedy felt it was an important first step to peace.

There was so much more he wanted to do. But the shots that rang out in Dallas put an end to all his dreams.

America lost a leader. A family lost a husband and a father. And no one knew why.

# Arrest

*November 22, 1963. Dallas, Texas.*

Who shot the President? That is what everyone wants to know.

Right away the police and the F.B.I. start looking for the answer. They question the hundreds of shocked, frightened people who saw the shooting.

Where did the shots come from? Some heard gunfire from in front of the President's car. Police hurry toward a railroad bridge and a grassy hill. They search for clues, but they find nothing.

Others say the shots came from behind the President's car. A man points to a building. It is a warehouse called the Texas School Book Depository. He says he saw a man in a sixth-floor window. A man with a rifle.

Here is the Texas School Book Depository. Was the President shot from the sixth-floor window?

Police race inside. They climb to the sixth floor. No one is there. But near an open window they find three bullet shells and, hidden close by, a rifle. Less than an hour after the shooting police believe they have found the murder weapon.

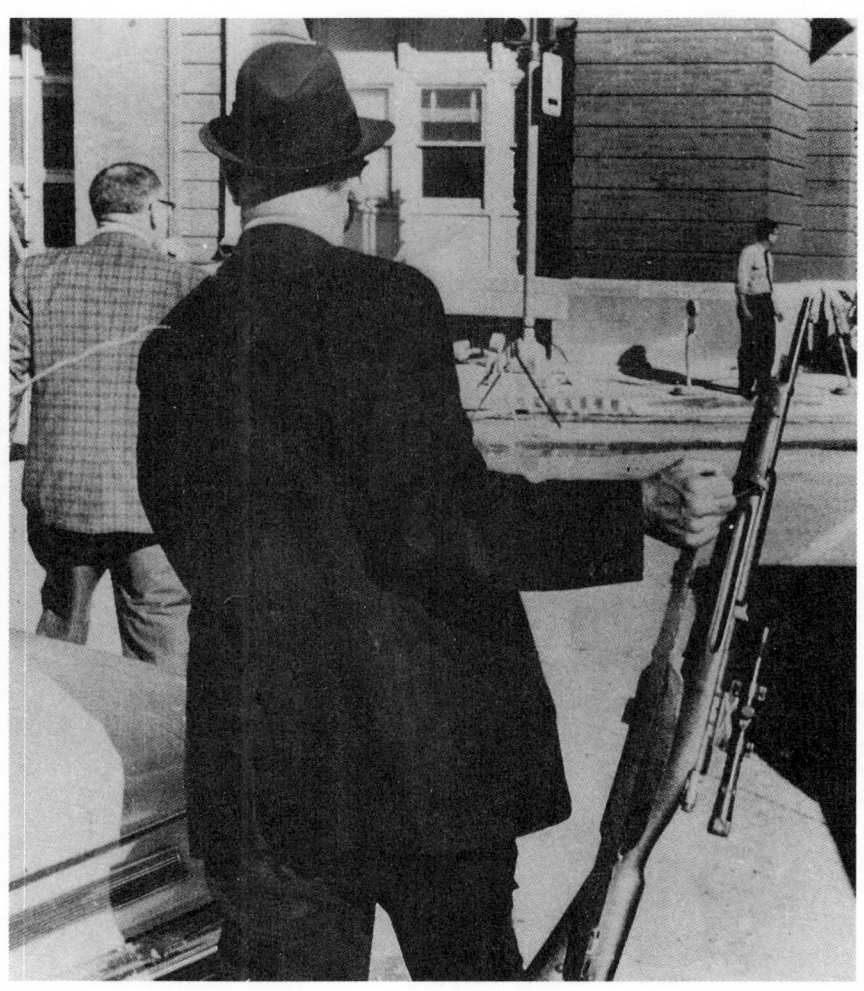

A Dallas detective holds the rifle that may have killed the President.

Just as the rifle is found, there is more shocking news. A Dallas policeman has been shot and killed a few miles from the warehouse. He was shot by a man he had stopped to question. Could this have something to do with the shooting of President Kennedy?

A description of the policeman's killer goes out on TV and radio. He is about thirty years old...slender, with black hair.... He has a gun.

A salesman in a Dallas shoe store hears the broadcast. He notices a man who fits the description standing just outside his store. The man turns away when a police car passes—as though he is trying to hide. Is he the one the police are looking for?

The salesman decides to follow the man. Carefully he trails behind. The man walks to a movie theater. The ticket seller is not there. The man goes inside anyway, without paying.

The salesman decides to call the police. In minutes police cars surround the theater. The lights are switched on. The salesman points out the man. He pulls a gun. He struggles. But finally he is under arrest.

The man's name is Lee Harvey Oswald. The police take him to the station. And they get a surprise. The police chief is looking for a man who works at the warehouse where the rifle was found. This man disappeared right after President Kennedy was shot. His name? Lee Harvey Oswald.

The police make another discovery. They learn the name of the man who owns the rifle found in the warehouse. Lee Harvey Oswald.

Reporters question Lee Harvey Oswald.

Is he the President's killer?

Oswald is questioned. He says, "I didn't shoot anybody."

But the police are sure he did. Lee Harvey Oswald is charged with the murder of President John F. Kennedy. Newspapers, TV, and radio carry the news everywhere.

Some of the facts of Oswald's life come out. He is an unhappy man. He has few friends. He has trouble getting and keeping jobs. He doesn't like the American government. Once he even went to live in the Soviet Union. He meant to stay, but he wasn't happy there, either. He came back to the United States.

Why would this man kill the President? There is no clear answer.

And Lee Harvey Oswald never gets to tell his side of the story.

On Sunday Oswald is to be moved to the county jail. Over a hundred people crowd into the station. Police. Reporters. Newscasters. They all want a look at Oswald. "Here he comes!" someone shouts. The room is bright with the glare of TV cameras. The crowd moves forward. Suddenly a man pushes through. A gun is in his hand. He shouts, "You killed the President, you rat!" He fires one shot, and Oswald falls to the ground. Within two hours Lee Harvey Oswald is dead.

It is almost too much to believe. The man accused of killing the President has been killed himself—in a room full of police and in front of millions of television viewers. Never in history has a crime been witnessed by so many people.

Jack Ruby is the name of Lee Harvey Oswald's killer. He owns two Dallas night clubs and is friendly with many policemen. No one is sure how he got into the station.

The Dallas police say the case of the President's murder is now closed.

They are very wrong.

This shocking photograph captures the exact moment Jack Ruby shot Lee Harvey Oswald.

# Saying Good-bye

*November 25, 1963. Washington, D.C.*

It is a cold day. But hundreds of people stand quietly outside the White House. Crowds have been there all through the night.

A million people line the streets of Washington, D.C. More than one hundred million across the country stay by their radios and television sets. President John F. Kennedy will be buried today. In one way or another almost every American is trying to say good-bye.

John Kennedy's coffin is carried past the White House.

Jacqueline Kennedy, dressed all in black, walks slowly toward St. Matthew's Cathedral. That is where a service for the President will be held. Mrs. Kennedy does not cry. But her face is full of sadness. The President's brothers, Bobby and Ted, walk beside her.

A car nearby carries the President's children, Caroline and John Jr. The President's sisters and mother are there too. So are kings, queens, and leaders from almost one hundred countries around the world.

Jacqueline Kennedy walks with the President's brothers, Bobby (who is on the left) and Ted.

President Kennedy's coffin is covered with an American flag. It rests on a black wagon pulled by six gray horses. A black horse without a rider prances behind them. Empty boots are turned backward in the stirrups. This stands for a leader who has died.

Army bands play slow, sad marches. But sometimes there is only the sound of muffled drums and horses' hooves. The crowds are very quiet. Some people cry softly.

Finally the coffin reaches the cathedral, and the family disappears inside.

People all over America take this time to show their own sadness. Bells are rung. Candles are lit in windows.

In many cities traffic stops for a few minutes. Trains do not leave. Planes do not take off. Ships stop, and sailors throw wreaths of flowers into the sea.

Many Americans go to their own churches and temples. Others bow their heads and pray wherever they are.

At the end of the service Mrs. Kennedy and her children wait at the bottom of the church steps. As the President's coffin is carried past, Mrs. Kennedy whispers to John Jr. He raises his hand in a salute. Today is John's third birthday. It is hard to imagine a sadder one.

John Jr. salutes as his father's coffin passes.

The children go home to the White House, but the rest of the Kennedy family moves on. The coffin, the marchers, and a long line of black cars go to Arlington National Cemetery in Virginia.

On a beautiful hillside John F. Kennedy is buried. The funeral is almost over. There is just one last thing to do. Mrs. Kennedy has asked that an eternal flame be placed near her husband's grave—a flame that will burn forever. She lights the torch. Then it is time to go.

## Mystery

President Kennedy is gone. President Johnson has taken his place. People want to put this terrible tragedy behind them. But there are questions America wants answered.

Could the shooting have been prevented? Could the President's life have been saved? Suppose the top had been on the car? Suppose the President's doctor had been nearby? What if Secret Service agents had been closer?

There are no answers. But today a president never rides in an open car. The roads his car will take are kept secret. America learned from John Kennedy's death.

People have other kinds of questions too. Was Lee Harvey Oswald really guilty? Did he kill the President? Did he do it all on his own?

Three other presidents have been shot and killed. Abraham Lincoln. James Garfield. William McKinley.

Abraham Lincoln

James Garfield

William McKinley

But the gunmen shot them from up close. Crowds of people saw the killers clearly. And each of the killers confessed his crime.

The killing of President Kennedy was different. The President was shot from far away.

The gunman was hidden. No one confessed to the crime.

Had Oswald lived, he would have gone to trial. Many more facts would have come out. Now that is impossible. But still, the American people want the truth. Who shot the President?

President Johnson decides the U.S. government must investigate the killing. He asks seven important men to find out what happened. The group is called the Warren Commission, after its leader, Supreme Court Chief Justice Earl Warren.

There are many clues. There is the rifle, the bullets, the doctors' reports on the President's wounds. There are the hundreds of witnesses to the shooting. And all the people who knew Lee Harvey Oswald and Jack Ruby. There is even a home movie by a man named Abraham Zapruder. Zapruder was filming the President's visit to Dallas, and his camera was on Kennedy at the very instant he was shot.

Here are some of the pictures from Abraham Zapruder's home movie.

The Warren Commission begins its investigation. Could the President have been shot from the warehouse? F.B.I. experts act out the crime to make sure it is possible. How good a shot was Oswald? The commission has his Army records checked to find out. Did the shots come from anywhere else? Witnesses tell the commission all they saw and heard that terrible day. The work goes on and on.

As months pass, the memory of President Kennedy seems to become more and more important to Americans. Everywhere schools and streets and parks are named after him. Millions of people come to visit his grave.

Then, almost a year after the President's death, the Warren Report is ready. It is almost nine hundred pages long. With it go nearly twenty thousand more pages with the words of witnesses, doctors, and police experts.

The Warren Report says that Lee Harvey Oswald killed President Kennedy and that he did it alone.

But some people do not believe the report. To them all the hundreds of clues are like pieces in a giant jigsaw puzzle. And the Warren Commission has jammed the pieces together when they really don't fit. They feel the Warren Commission decided Oswald was guilty even before the investigation began.

Many agree that Oswald probably did shoot the President—but not alone. They think there was a *conspiracy*—a secret plan that involved more people. They believe there had to be a second gunman.

Lee Harvey Oswald was in the warehouse *behind* the President. But most witnesses thought the shots came from the grassy hill *in front of* the President. Could another gunman have been hiding there?

The report is questioned for other reasons too. The Zapruder film shows that both the President and Governor Connally were hit within two seconds. But Oswald's cheap, old-fashioned rifle couldn't fire that quickly. The commission decided the two men probably were wounded by a single bullet from Oswald's gun. Governor Connally himself is sure they were not hit by the same bullet. Doesn't it make more sense, people ask, that more than one gunman was shooting?

The film also shows the President's head

Where did the shots come from? This diagram shows the President's car, the grassy hill in front of it, and the warehouse behind.

jerk back as he was hit. Some scientists insist that proves he was shot from the front.

And what about the Dallas doctors? Right after the shooting they said the President's wounds showed he had been hit from the front. The doctors later changed their minds, but they could have been right in the first place.

Some people believe the truth has been covered up. Suppose the real killers tried to make Oswald look guilty? Suppose they got Jack Ruby to shoot Oswald to make sure the facts would never come out. Then Oswald would get the blame, and the real killers would go free.

Many of the people who disagree with the Warren Report start investigations on their own. Some of them give speeches. Others write books and articles about their ideas.

More and more Americans begin to wonder. Are these people right? What is the truth?

In 1976 Congress opens a new investigation

into the death of John F. Kennedy. After more than two years they decide that Lee Harvey Oswald did fire the shot that killed the President. But they say there probably *was* a secret plan to murder him—a plan that involved other people. And there probably *was* a second gunman.

Does this solve the mystery?

Not really. Some people disagree with this new report. They believe the Warren Commission.

Some still feel there is no real proof that Oswald was guilty at all.

Others agree with the new investigation, but they want to know much more. If there was another gunman, who was he? If there was a secret plan, who was behind it? Who wanted John Kennedy killed? And why?

People will wonder about the death of President Kennedy many years from now. Someday the mystery may even be solved.

But the Americans who loved him remember the man more than the mystery surrounding his death. They remember John F. Kennedy's life, and a time of hope for America.